W9-BZT-209

SUBWAYS

by Mary Winget

Lerner Publications Company • Minneapolis

For Tiernan, Sebastian, and Great Grandpa Mueller

Text copyright © 2007 by Lerner Publications Company

Lerner Publications Company
A division of Lerner Publishing Group
241 First Avenue North
Minneapolis, MN 55401 U.S.A.

Website address: www.lernerbooks.com

Words in **bold** type are explained in a glossary on page 30.

Library of Congress Cataloging-in-Publication Data

Winget, Mary.
    Subways / by Mary Winget.
       p. cm. — (Pull ahead books)
    Includes index.
    ISBN-13: 978-0-8225-6418-8 (lib. bdg. : alk. paper)
    ISBN-10: 0-8225-6418-1 (lib. bdg. : alk. paper)
    1. Subways—Juvenile literature. I. Title. II. Series.
TF845.W56 2007
625.4'2—dc22   2006007061

Manufactured in the United States of America
1 2 3 4 5 6 — JR — 12 11 10 09 08 07

Whoosh! What was that rushing by
so fast?

It was a subway. Subways are special trains that run in **tunnels**. The tunnels are underground.

Too many cars and buses make city streets crowded. Traffic moves slowly. How will people get to places on time?

People can take subways. Subways never get stuck in traffic. How do people get on subways?

Riders must go to a subway station.
They pay a **fare** for a ticket. The fare
is the price of a subway ride.

Riders swipe their tickets in a slot. Then they go through a **turnstile**.

People go down stairs to get to the **platform**. They wait on the platform for a subway to come.

Look! The subway is coming. You can see its light coming through the tunnel.

Stay back from the edge! Wait until
the subway stops moving.

When the subway stops, the doors slide open. People get off the subway.

New riders get on the subway. The doors slide closed. The subway is full of people. Where will they all sit?

Subways have many seats. They can carry lots of riders.

Some riders find empty seats to sit in. Other riders have to stand. They hold on to handles or poles.

The subway begins to move. It goes
into a dark tunnel. Bright lights stay on
inside the subway.

Subways run on tracks. There are usually two sets of tracks.

Subways on one track move in one direction. Subways on the other track move in a different direction.

Subways have many **cars**. Each car is linked to the next car.

The first car on a subway is the railcar.
The railcar pulls the rest of the subway.

An **operator** sits in the railcar. The operator controls how fast or slow the subway moves.

What makes subways go? They get
power from **electricity**. Subway tracks
have three rails. The third rail carries
electricity.

Electricity moves from the third rail to the railcar.

This subway is arriving at a station.
Signs at each station tell riders where
they are.

It's time for these people to get off the subway. They go up the stairs to the street.

Traffic on the street is still slow and
crowded. But subway riders don't
have to worry about traffic.

Subways make it easy to travel in crowded cities. Subways get riders to places on time!

Fun Facts about Subways

- The first subway opened in London, England, in 1863. Its track was four miles long.

- New York City's first real subway opened on October 27, 1904. Church bells rang, and factory whistles blew in celebration.

- More than 4.3 million people ride subways in New York City every day.

- In the United States, many cities have subways. Boston, Chicago, Los Angeles, New York, and Washington, D.C., all have subways.

- In Tokyo, Japan, subway stations have huge, underground shopping malls.

Parts of a Subway

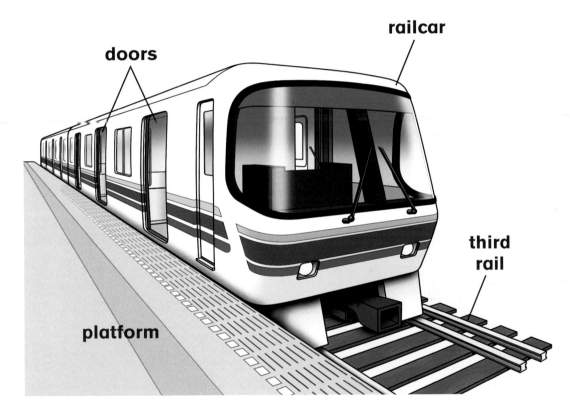

doors

railcar

third rail

platform

Glossary

cars: parts of a subway where people ride

electricity: energy used to move subways

fare: the cost of a subway ride

operator: the person who runs a subway

platform: an area in a subway station where people wait for subways

tunnels: underground paths that subways take

turnstile: a gate that riders go through to get on a subway

More about Subways

Check out these books and websites to find out more about subways.

Books

Hill, Lee Sullivan. *Trains.* Minneapolis: Lerner Publications Company, 2003.
This book has information about trains and how they work.

Weitzman, David. *A Subway for New York.* New York: Farrar, Straus and Giroux, 2005.
This book has more about subways and their history.

Websites

Public Transportation Safety Kids Page
http://www.nysgtsc.state.ny.us/Kids/kid-tran.htm
This website from the state of New York has lots of information about public transportation safety, including a section on subways.

Big Apple History—Subways
http://pbskids.org/bigapplehistory/building/topic20.html
Find out more about the history of New York City's subway system through this website from the Educational Broadcasting Corporation.

Index

cars, 19, 20

doors, 12, 13

poles, 15
power, 22–23

railcar, 20, 21, 23

seats, 14, 15
stairs, 9, 25
station, 7, 24, 28

ticket, 7, 8
tracks, 17, 18, 22
traffic, 5, 6, 26
tunnels, 4, 10, 16

Photo Acknowledgments

The photographs in this book appear with the permission of: © Art Stein/ZUMA/CORBIS, cover; © MedioImages/Getty Images, p. 3; © Image Source/Getty Images, p. 4; © Travis Lindquist/Getty Images, p. 5; © Doug Menuez/Photodisc Green/Getty Images, p. 6; © Richard T. Nowitz/CORBIS, p. 7; © age fotostock/SuperStock, pp. 8, 19, 26; © STAN HONDA/AFP/Getty Images, pp. 9, 11; © Paul A. Souders/CORBIS, p. 10; © Ramin Talaie/CORBIS, p. 12; © Junko Kimura/Getty Images, p. 13; © Alan Schein Photography/CORBIS, p. 14; © Paula Bronstein/Getty Images, p. 15; © PORNCHAI KIT-TIWONGSAKUL/AFP/Getty Images, p. 16; © James P. Blair/CORBIS, p. 17; © Lester Lefkowitz/CORBIS, p. 18; © Colin Garratt; Milepost 92½/CORBIS, p. 20; © Frédérik Astier/Sygma/CORBIS, p. 21; © Louis K. Meisel Gallery, Inc./CORBIS, p. 22; © Robert Holmes/CORBIS, p. 23; © Stephen Chernin/Getty Images, p. 24; © New Regency/20th Century Fox/The Kobal Collection/Bailey, K C, p. 25; © Royalty-Free/CORBIS, p. 27. Illustration on p. 29 by © Laura Westlund/Independent Picture Service.